Original title:
Life, Laughter, and a Latte

Copyright © 2025 Creative Arts Management OÜ
All rights reserved.

Author: Maya Livingston
ISBN HARDBACK: 978-1-80566-026-2
ISBN PAPERBACK: 978-1-80566-321-8

Dreamy Drizzles

A morning mist with frothy whim,
Drizzles dance on the edge of brim.
Frogs in jackets hop to meet,
The coffee's warmth and banana seat.

Sugar sprinkles twirl and play,
As giggles bubble, bright and gay.
A splash of cream, a dash of zest,
In magic mugs, we feel the best.

Sauntering Through Sips

Wandering through the fragrant lanes,
With liquid joy in joyous reigns.
The world a swirl of vivid hues,
Each cup unfolds delightful news.

Sipping dreams in morning's glow,
Where every drop puts on a show.
With playful bubbles, laughter swirls,
As coffee wonders twirl and twirls.

The Spontaneity of Steaming Cups

A clatter, a whirr, the kettle sings,
As chubby kittens stretch their wings.
Join the frolic, pour it free,
Catch the whims of jubilee!

Each sip a hug, each mug a friend,
Melodies through the steam ascend.
Together we toast to joyous flips,
Unplanned moments in frothy sips.

Glee in the Grind

The grinder whirrs, the beans take flight,
A playful twist from day to night.
With quirks and quirks, our thoughts unwind,
In every brew, sweet chaos find.

Drip by drip, the stories blend,
A swirl of wonders without end.
In each sip, a chuckle frames,
As coffee cheers and giggles reign.

Celebration in Every Sip

In the mug, a swirl of cheer,
Each sip, a giggle that's near.
Frothy tales that dance and play,
Turning blues into bright array.

With sprinkles of joy on the top,
We toast to moments that never stop.
A dash of whimsy, a splash of fun,
In every gulp, we've just begun.

Flavors of a Fulfilling Day

Morning's brew, a playful tease,
Whispers of sweetness in the breeze.
Every sip, a story unfolds,
Tickling the senses, as it molds.

The sun beams down, a wink so bright,
With every drop, the heart takes flight.
A blend of joy, like sunshine rays,
Perked up spirits, in bright arrays.

Spills of Joy

A little tip, a tiny spill,
Who knew chaos could thrill?
Laughter bubbles, the floor's a mess,
But in this clatter, there's happiness.

Each drop that falls, a giggling sound,
In the chorus of clinks, love is found.
From cups to laughter, the joy spills wide,
In this delightful, caffeinated ride.

Heartstrings and Coffee Cups

With every sip, our spirits unite,
Jokes shared over the morning light.
The warmth in hand, a bond so tight,
Frothy smiles that shine so bright.

In cozy corners, we find our place,
Stories brewed with laughter's grace.
A hug in a cup, a sprinkle of wit,
Together we thrive, we never quit.

Brushstrokes of Warmth

With a splash of cream, the day begins,
Juggling dreams, while wearing grins.
Sugar sprinkles like confetti bright,
 Sip and twirl into morning light.

Each drop a giggle, each swirl a tease,
Witty thoughts floating like autumn leaves.
A mug of cheer, a hint of spice,
 Sipping joy, who needs advice?

The Palette of Percolation

In a swirl of brown, the world takes shape,
Mirthful sips, no room for drape.
Mugs laugh together, they share their tales,
While steam rises like happy wails.

Frothy dreams dance, a playful sight,
Mocha giggles burst with delight.
Colorful sips bring smiles to face,
With every sip, we embrace the grace.

Expecting the Unexpected

A splash here, a splash there, it's quite a show,
Spontaneous giggles in every flow.
Surprises bubble, just like the brew,
Stirred with whimsy, it's all brand new.

A spoon bounces lightly in playful glee,
Creating a buzz like a bumblebee.
Puns in the air make the spouts sing,
Life's little joys are the best of bling.

Embracing Warmth and Whimsy

Cup in hand, I stroll through the fun,
Chasing echoes of jokes, one by one.
Sugar swirls with a pinch of the odd,
In this quirky concoction, I find my nod.

A giggle erupts with every taste,
No room for gloom in this bubbling haste.
Sip by sip, the warmth takes root,
In the froth of humor, I'm resolute.

Cheery Conversations with Cream

In a café bright, where the mugs gleam,
Funny tales flow like a bubbling stream.
With a sprinkle of joy, and a twist of a grin,
Each sip's a giggle, let the fun begin.

The barista jests with a wink in his eye,
His frothy creations make the dull clouds fly.
With every froth swirl, a new joke unfurls,
Caffeine and chuckles, oh how the heart twirls!

We toast to the moments, both silly and sweet,
Matching our laughter with every heartbeat.
Conversation bubbles, like cream on the top,
In this cozy corner, we'll never stop.

A scone with a smirk, it's a whimsical feast,
With pastries that giggle, we're humor's least beast.
From giggling lattes to sassy sweet tarts,
This haven of laughter will warm our hearts.

Bridging Hearts with Coffee

A steaming cup in hand so bright,
Bridges built with every bite,
Conversations swirl in the air,
Laughter erupts without a care.

Brewed just right, a magic spell,
We share our tales, oh how they swell,
Between the sips and silly grins,
Friendship grows, and joy begins.

The Heart of Every Gathering

Around the table, stories flow,
With every sip, new friendships grow,
Mugs are lifted, cheers abound,
In this warmth, our joy is found.

Cups clink softly, hearts beat loud,
In this place, we gather proud,
Witty banter fills the night,
With every sip, our spirits light.

Sip by Sip

Frothy foam on a sunny day,
Every sip takes woes away,
Smiles peek above the rim,
In this moment, we all swim.

With each cup, a laugh we share,
Funny faces, love laid bare,
Sips of warmth bring us near,
Laughter dances, joy is here.

Spirited Brews and Shared Stories

Dark roast tales steeped with cheer,
Every story brings us near,
Whimsical dreams in a java cup,
Each new sip, we lift it up.

Silly jokes and frothy frolic,
Every moment slightly chaotic,
As we sip and laugh anew,
With every brew, my heart says true.

Morning Brews and Mirth

The sun peeks through the sleepy haze,
A mug awaits to start the day.
With frothy swirls and whispers bright,
We giggle at the morning light.

Each sip a chuckle, each taste a cheer,
With every gulp, we conquer fear.
The steam rises like playful ghosts,
In our cozy nook, we're true hosts.

Whispers of Happiness in a Cup

A cup of warmth in our hands we hold,
Like secret stories waiting to unfold.
With every sip, a joke is born,
And all our troubles feel just worn.

The world outside moves at a pace,
But in this sip, we find our grace.
Laughter bubbles like the brew,
It's here we know just what to do.

Sips of Joy and Sunshine

The morning glow dances in our eyes,
We share a drink, watch the clouds rise.
With playful banter, we lift our cups,
As if the world has forgotten its ups.

Each slosh and splash feels like a game,
In this merry swirl, we chase our fame.
Sipping joy with every drip,
Life's silly moments on this trip.

The Art of Steaming Smiles

In the café corner, we plot and scheme,
Over frothy drinks, we sip and dream.
A touch of foam, a sprinkle of spice,
Our laughter frosts the chilly ice.

Each cup's a canvas, each sip a stroke,
In swirls of warmth, we've found our joke.
With smiles like cream on our happy brew,
We toast to the fun in all that we do.

A Symphony of Sips

In a café where dreams arise,
Cups jingle like tiny chimes,
A barista's dance, a grand surprise,
As frothy clouds spin in perfect rhymes.

Whispers swirl in mocha air,
Jokes percolate, laughter brews,
Each sip a spark, mischief to share,
With every flavor, joy ensues.

Moments Poured with Care

Steam rises like giggles in the room,
With every cup, a joke unfolds,
Stirring joy amidst the doom,
As stories brew, the heart beholds.

A sprinkle of spice, a dollop of cream,
Each swig ignites a playful fight,
A sip of warmth, a daydream theme,
As taste buds dance in pure delight.

Tasting Together

Two mugs clink, like joyful chords,
With every slurp, a chuckle bright,
Savoring sips, a friendship hoards,
In this café, mischief takes flight.

Smiles bloom with every taste,
Laughter bubbles, the world's in tune,
Hours dissolve, with no waste,
As we toast beneath the moon.

Warm Melodies and Mugfuls

Chatter flows like rivers wide,
Caffeine dreams in silly streams,
In every mug, a giggle hides,
As innocence dances in our dreams.

A coffee note, a chocolate lick,
Jokes spiral in frothy swirls,
With every sip, we pick and stick,
To forgo frowns and twirl our curls.

Brews that Bind

In that cozy corner, smiles ignite,
Coffee spills stories, oh what a sight!
Laughter erupts like steam from the cup,
With every sip, we just can't get enough.

Mugs clink like bells, a cheerful parade,
Brewed friendships blossom, never to fade.
Jokes swirling around like sugar in cream,
Together we stumble, but always a team.

Cosy Connections

Warmth in the air, vanilla scents dance,
Chasing our worries, giving joy a chance.
Faces aglow in the soft, gentle light,
In this snug little spot, the world feels just right.

Banter like bubbles, we giggle and tease,
Comfort found here, like a favorite fleece.
With every sip shared, our troubles take flight,
In the heart of the moment, everything's bright.

Happiness Steeped in Warmth

Steam rises gently, a fog of delight,
Cup in our hands, everything feels right.
Sip by sip, the worries all drift,
Shared smiles and tales are the perfect gift.

Swirls of rich chocolate, our favorite blend,
Nectar of joy that we happily send.
In the chatter and clatter, we find our zen,
Each sip a reunion, again and again.

Sweet Serendipity

Once upon a time in a café quite small,
Strangers turned friends, over brews shared by all.
Laughter like confetti, a joy-filled parade,
Sweet serendipity in every charade.

Sips that bring chuckles, a whimsical tease,
Life's little wonders, as simple as cheese.
In the warmth of our mugs, the spark we all find,
Together we dance, with the brew that's designed.

The Brewed Connection

In a small café where dreams take flight,
People gather, their smiles so bright.
With cups in hand, they share their tales,
A swirl of flavors, where laughter prevails.

Each sip a giggle, each gulp a cheer,
Brewed concoctions that draw us near.
A splash of cream, a sprinkle of fun,
In this cozy nook, we all are one.

Vibrancy in the Everyday

Morning sun spills a golden blend,
With waking hopes that never end.
A foam art heart or a silly cat,
Every sip makes us smile, imagine that!

The barista's jokes, with puns stacked high,
Make the ordinary soar, oh my!
Under the spell of aromas so sweet,
Each bite of pastry, a tiny treat.

Mugs and Memories

In mismatched mugs with stories untold,
Are moments of warmth, memories to hold.
The chatter bounces like beans in a pot,
With each silly blunder, we laugh at the lot.

From spilled drinks to crumbs on the floor,
Every misstep just opens the door.
To friendships brewed, strong and near,
In this funny joint, there's nothing to fear.

Euphoria in Every Drop

As steam rises up, so do our woes,
With a smile and a sip, how the happiness grows!
Chocolate drizzles and whipped cream clouds,
In this parade of flavors, laughter shrouds.

A clumsy dance while stirring the mix,
Our spirits lift with every little fix.
An elbow bump, a giggle, a cheer,
In every warm cup, joy draws us near.

Golden Hours in a Cup

The sun spills warmth, a perfect blend,
Coffee swirls as smiles extend.
Silly thoughts bounce in the air,
Joyful moments, nothing to bear.

Chasing dreams with frothy cream,
A wink, a nudge, laughter's theme.
Sips of cheer dance on the tongue,
In this cup, we're forever young.

Lifting Spirits with Each Sip

The morning brew, a little joke,
Awakens cheer like playful smoke.
With every gulp, the giggles grow,
Funny stories start to flow.

Caffeine fixes grumps in line,
Jokes percolate with every vine.
A splash of fun in every pour,
Raising spirits, who needs more?

Echoes of Laughter

In corners bright, where friends convene,
Mirth erupts, a lively scene.
With cups held tight, we share our days,
In chuckles sweet, joy softly sways.

A gentle tease, the laughter rings,
In the noise, the heart takes wings.
Every chuckle, a spark of light,
It paints the gray and makes it bright.

Percolating Positivity

Beans collide, a force divine,
Brews of happiness intertwine.
Swirling flavors mix with glee,
A frothy smile, oh, can't you see?

With cada sip, the world's a joke,
Amidst the steam, we laugh and poke.
The cup's alive with tales to share,
In every sip, we shed our care.

Glimmers of Glee

In the corner, feathers fly,
With a latte mustache, oh my!
Sipping dreams with a twist of fate,
As the giggles orchestrate.

Bubbly hiccups fill the air,
Chasing clouds without a care.
Froth may drip on my new dress,
But who needs grace? It's pure success!

Juggling thoughts like coffee beans,
Twisting tales in silly scenes.
Spin the chair, I feel so free,
In this moment, just let it be.

Glimmers spark in every sip,
Laughter dances, life's a trip.
Through frothy hearts and warm embrace,
Happiness found in this wild space.

A Toast to the Ordinary

We raise our mugs and sing a cheer,
To mirthful moments gathered here.
With quirks and smiles, we take a stand,
In a café, hand in hand.

A spill, a giggle, what a plight,
Hiccups burst in soft twilight.
Whipped cream clouds atop each head,
Who knew joy was this widespread?

Sips collide and stories blend,
Every jest, a new best friend.
In ordinary places, laughter wakes,
As we revel in our coffee breaks.

Toast the days both hot and cold,
Little treasures, purest gold.
In simple things, we find delight,
With every laugh, our spirits light.

The Joyful Grind

Buzzing beans in morning light,
Steaming mugs brew pure delight.
Each drip echoes laughter's sound,
In this rhythm, joy is found.

Chasing dreams with sugar sprinkles,
Stirring up the fun as it twinkles.
Three spoonfuls of whimsy, a dash of glee,
What's more playful than a caffeine spree?

Witty banter breaks the dawn,
With every sip, we cheer and yawn.
Latte art and perky smiles,
Making magic out of miles.

The world spins in caffeinated cheer,
Let's dance our way till the next career.
In the grind, we'll find our way,
With each laugh, we seize the day.

Flavors of Friendship

Like caramel swirls on a lazy morn,
We mix our stories, never worn.
With each sip, the tales unfold,
In flavors rich and laughter bold.

A dash of mischief, a sprinkle of fun,
Brewing joy till the day is done.
Chocolate chips and shared delight,
Brings warmth to every chilly night.

We toast to chaos with cups held high,
Crack a joke, let laughter fly.
In this blend, our hearts conjoin,
Creating bonds that brightly shine.

Here's to moments steeped with cheer,
Knowing friendship's always near.
In every taste, the spirit beams,
As we savor all our dreams.

Serendipity Served Hot

Woke up late, a sputter and spat,
Forgot my shoes, now where's my cat?
Coffee's brewing, will it survive?
Pour it quick, I need that vibe!

Muffins flying, a surprise delight,
A squirrel scampers, what a sight!
Chasing crumbs, a dance so grand,
Laughter echoes across the land.

The day unfolds, a twisty road,
With spills and thrills, I wear the load.
Yet every blunder, every slip,
Turns my frown to a joyful quip.

At dusk I sip, a cup so warm,
With friends that gather, a perfect swarm.
We'll toast to chaos, to silly strife,
In every sip, there's a taste of life!

The Warmth of a Shared Moment

A table set with mugs all round,
Chatter bubbles, joy is found.
We share our tales, the old and new,
With every sip, our laughter grew.

A tiny spill, it lands on me,
We giggle softly, oh what glee!
A dash of cream, a sprinkle of cheer,
The warmth we share, it draws us near.

In every clink of ceramic dear,
We find the stories we hold near.
A talk of dreams, both wild and bold,
With every word a heart unfolds.

As daylight fades, our cups run low,
Yet in our hearts, the memories glow.
We'll chase this magic, come what may,
In moments shared, we find our way!

Tasting Joy from the Bottom of a Cup

In the bottom of my cup, secrets dwell,
A swirl of flavor, a cozy spell.
Each sip brings giggles, a twinkling eye,
What mischief awaits, oh me, oh my!

Friends by my side, tales interlace,
Spinning like sugar, all in good grace.
A shot of espresso, a dash of grin,
We sip and savor, let the fun begin.

With crumbs of pastries stuck to my cheek,
I make up stories, silly and cheeky.
In this little café, time stands still,
Just laughter and warmth, a perfect thrill.

So raise your cups, a toast to the day,
To misadventures that come our way.
With every drop, joy flows anew,
In this warm haven, just me and you!

A Blend of Happiness and Cream

Whisking froth, like clouds of cheer,
A little dance, come join me here!
Sugar sprinkles in endless supply,
With every giggle, emotions fly.

Caught in a swirl, our laughter blends,
Every mishap feels like a trend.
Creamy waves and stories collide,
In this moment, our hearts abide.

Sip by sip, our spirits rise,
With every chuckle, the world feels wise.
A foamy heart drawn in the cup,
Invites the joy to bubble up.

So let's embrace the silly and sweet,
With friends around, oh, it's a treat!
For in this blend, we find our dream,
In every sip, we share our beam!

Moments Between the Sips

In a café buzzing with glee,
A jester spilled his tea.
Laughter erupted, oh what a sight,
As foam took flight in pure delight.

Friends gathered round with eager grins,
Sharing tales of funny wins.
Muffins tumbled, croissants flew,
The barista laughed, fetching a brew.

At a table strewn with crumbs,
Crazy dances and playful hums.
A glimpse of joy in every sip,
As bubbles danced with each cool dip.

The clock ticked on, but time stood still,
With every sip, we felt the thrill.
Moments cherished, secrets shared,
In this place, we never scared.

Tasting Tomorrow

A sip of mystery in a cup,
It whispers softly, 'Drink me up!'
With every taste, a twist of fate,
What will happen? We just can't wait!

The sun spills in through windowpanes,
Casting shadows, leaving stains.
Laughter echoes through the space,
As syrup drips, we quicken pace.

Silly stories swirl with cream,
Each one weaves a little dream.
Foamy hats on cups so round,
In giggles, we all are bound.

Tomorrow's taste is brewed today,
With every chat, we find our way.
A hint of mischief in the air,
A journey flavored with happy flair.

Rich Flavors of Togetherness

Gathered here, the world feels bright,
Cup in hand, all feels right.
With each pour we build our tale,
Spicy, sweet, we can't fail.

The conversation flows like wine,
Every joke, a joyful sign.
Sprinkled laughter in a cup,
As the world spills its hiccups up.

A dash of cream, a hint of spice,
We raise our mugs, oh how nice!
Every gulp, a memory made,
In flavors where our hearts parade.

Friends forever, the bond is rich,
With every sip, we find our niche.
Jokes served hot, we feast on cheer,
In this brew, our truths appear.

Cradled in Comfort

In a corner snug, we sit tight,
A cozy spot, the mood is right.
With giggles bubbling like a pot,
Here we chase the joys we sought.

The aroma wraps us like a hug,
Each sip a whisper, each word a tug.
Sloppy cream and sugar swirls,
Our laughter's dance, a joyous whirl.

The clock hands dance, they spin and twirl,
As stories unravel, dream flags unfurl.
Slipping through time on a foam-filled wave,
Here, we find the warmth we crave.

In this embrace, the world melts away,
Comfort wrapped in a perfect play.
A moment shared over treats so fine,
Together we sip, together we shine.

Sips of Sunshine

The mugs are bright, a cheerful sight,
With frothy clouds, they take to flight.
I giggle as the cream swirls 'round,
  A joyous treat, in each sip found.

The jokes we trade, like sugar sweet,
They warm our hearts, and lift our feet.
We sip our dreams in playful glee,
  Beneath the sun, just you and me.

Whispers in the Foam

A whisper soft, in bubbles rise,
Each frothy swirl, a funny surprise.
Giggles dance on the edges fair,
As flavors mingle, filling the air.

We play with flavors, wild and bold,
The laughter brews, a tale retold.
The world outside fades away with the steam,
In warm embrace, we sip and dream.

Mirth in Every Mug

With every sip, a chuckle spills,
Creamy capers bring endless thrills.
What's brewing here is pure delight,
As friendship blooms in morning light.

A splash of joy in mugs of cheer,
With every drink, calamity near.
We toast to quirks, to all that's weird,
With coffee in hand, let's not be feared.

Warmth in Togetherness

In every cup, a warmth we find,
Shared moments rich, uniquely combined.
The humor flows, with every pour,
As laughter echoes, we crave for more.

So gather close, let's share our brew,
With clinking mugs, and hearts so true.
For in this space, where joy ignites,
Togetherness sparkles, our spirits take flight.

Flavorful Moments

In a cup of joy, we find delight,
Chocolate sprinkles on a sunny bite.
Friends gather round with chatter and cheer,
Sipping memories, year after year.

With every swirl, a story unfolds,
Warmth in our hearts, like hugs, it holds.
A dash of wit, a pinch of smiles,
In mugs of mirth, we travel for miles.

Carefree Hearts

Whipped cream clouds that dance on top,
Nonsense spills as we laugh and swap.
Giggling over froth like children at play,
Our worries vanish, just for today.

Each sip a tickle, a burst of glee,
A friendship brewed, wild and free.
With warmth in our cups, we raise a toast,
To moments like these, we cherish the most.

The Richness of Laughter in Every Sip

A swirl of flavors, a frothy delight,
Chuckle and cackle, from morning till night.
With a gentle sigh, we sip and we grin,
Creating a world where smiles begin.

The cream rises high, just like our jokes,
Spilling over, the joy invokes.
In each warm drink, a spark of cheer,
Echoes of laughter, oh so near.

Cardamom, Cocoa, and Coincidence

A sprinkle of spice in the blender's song,
Fortune favors those who laugh along.
Cocoa kisses the morning air,
In serendipity's weave, we find our share.

Mixing mishaps with a dash of glee,
Unexpected moments, just you and me.
In our sweet concoction, love brews bold,
Tales of whimsy and warmth to be told.

A Caffeine Canvas of Connection

Easel of colors, the cup comes alive,
Brewed with passion, our spirits thrive.
Each blend a brushstroke, each sip a hue,
Creating a masterpiece, just me and you.

Laughter splatters like paint on the wall,
In this café of dreams, we embrace it all.
A portrait of moments in steamy refrains,
Where the art of connection forever remains.

The Symphony of Steam and Cheer

In a cup of swirls and dreams,
We find the magic, or so it seems.
A frothy crown atop a brew,
Whispers secrets known to few.

With every sip, the giggles rise,
Like bubbles dancing in the skies.
A sprinkle of joy, a splash of glee,
Fills the air with harmony.

Jesters laugh in every pour,
Tales of laughter, never a bore.
A melody of warmth and fun,
Brightening days 'til they are done.

So raise your cup to silly times,
To silly jokes and wacky rhymes.
For in this drink, we find delight,
A frothy world, so merry and bright.

Frothy Encounters on a Quiet Street

On cobblestone, a tinkle rings,
As baristas dance and laughter sings.
A latte spills, a giggle shared,
Warmth ignites, we are prepared.

Two friends meet, their mugs collide,
With frothy jokes that won't subside.
A dash of cream, a splash of cheer,
With every sip, the world feels near.

The secret code of coffee talk,
Each wink, a chance for playful mock.
Under awnings where shadows play,
Beneath the sun, we greet the day.

As mugs run dry, so do our tears,
Of laughter's strength that conquers fears.
With grins that stretch from ear to ear,
On quiet streets, we spread our cheer.

Chasing Rainbows in a Beverage

In mugs of colors, swirling bright,
We sip and smile, pure delight.
A taste of cheer, a zing of lime,
Each gooey sip, a dash of rhyme.

Marshmallow clouds float on the foam,
With each hearty laugh, we feel at home.
Beneath blue skies or grayish hues,
There's joy to find in all we choose.

Geysers of giggles erupt on cue,
As secrets spill in every brew.
Sprinkled wishes and wishes on top,
In this cafe, we never stop.

Chasing flavors, painting the day,
With every drop, we dance and play.
So raise your glass to all things bright,
Together, we'll take flight tonight.

Mugfuls of Mirth and Memory

In every sip, a story brewed,
A memory wrapped in frothy food.
Laughter bubbles, joy awakes,
As moments blend, and time just breaks.

Time spent with friends—a heart's delight,
In cozy spots, where all feels right.
A dash of whimsy in steaming cups,
Pouring giggles, never shuts up.

With toasty hands and warming souls,
We share our dreams, we chase our goals.
A nod, a wink, with every stir,
As life's light dances, we concur.

So fill your mugs and join the show,
With each warm swig, let laughter flow.
Memories made, and joy we find,
In every brew, our hearts aligned.

Stirring Smiles

In a cup, adventures brew,
With a sprinkle of joy, it's true.
Each sip brings a giggle or two,
Oh, what mischief a mug can do!

Sugar swirls in a chaotic dance,
While foam rides high with a frothy romance.
Watch the tales unfold, take a chance,
In every swirl, imagination prance!

Whisking dreams like a playful breeze,
Laughter emerges like sweetness that frees.
How many giggles fit in a tease?
Sipping slowly, my soul's at ease.

A brew with spark and a twist of fate,
Chasing worries, never too late.
In this moment, it's truly great,
With cups in hand, we celebrate!

The Dance of Daybreak

At dawn's light, the pot sings bright,
Joking steam takes happy flight.
Nutty aromas tease the nose,
Sipping slow, the magic grows.

Conversations bubble, giggles shared,
Morning bliss, none can be spared.
The sun peeks in, with a cheerful cheer,
As coffee whispers, 'Come near, my dear!'

A swirl of cream, a dash of glee,
With each sip, a friendly decree.
Sip it quick, or let it float,
Giddy laughter is no afterthought!

The day begins with a silly spin,
Where silliness and sweetness meld within.
Join the dance, lose all the frowns,
In every cup, joy knows no bounds!

Blissful Brews

In cafes bright, the jests unfold,
With frothy caps, our hearts they hold.
A chuckle here, a chuckle there,
Oh, what laughter fills the air!

With every sip, a grin appears,
Tales of old bring the merry cheers.
Caffeine dreams ignite the fun,
Watch the giggles burst and run!

Creamy delights, a funny plea,
Savoring moments, just you and me.
The world outside may be in strife,
But in this cup, we savor life!

As cups get empty, spirits soar,
With promises of more and more.
A splash of joy, a dash of cheer,
In every brew, our hearts grow near!

Conversations Over Cream

Gather round for tales untold,
With laughter wrapped in cups of gold.
The cream cascades like a flowing jest,
In every drop, we find our quest.

Chatting 'bout dreams, our smiles align,
Each yawn turns bright with a sip of wine.
Sweet nothings swirl in the foamy art,
Over mugs, we pour out our heart!

As flavors dance, the giggles grow,
We toast to moments, let the joy flow.
A sip of this, and a laugh from that,
In our café corner, joy is where it's at!

With cream on our lips and smiles so wide,
We share our stories, side by side.
In this haven, worries refrain,
Over cups of delight, it's always sunshine rain!

The Art of Morning Rituals

Awake, the sun begins to peek,
A dance with socks, two left feet,
Coffee brews with a happy glee,
The cat's strange looks, so much to see.

Toaster pops, light's a fresh spread,
Burnt toast gives my heart a dread.
Sips of warmth, like hugs in a cup,
Laughter bubbles as I mix it up.

The mirror cracks a playful grin,
Mismatched pajamas, where to begin?
Spilling dreams with toast on my lap,
Giggles rise, oh what a mishap!

Outside, the world begins to stir,
Neighbors pass, each with a purr.
A morning crew of quirky souls,
We share our woes, it never gets old.

Chasing Clouds and Coffee

With dreams as fluffy as the cream,
I chase the clouds in morning's beam,
The barista winks, a mischievous jest,
Coffee beans dance, they know best.

Cup in hand, I wander to skies,
Imagining tales where laughter flies.
A sip, a splash, oh what delight,
The sun takes center, shining bright.

Giggles swirl in every sip,
Life's a circus, all on a trip.
Clouds wear hats, a whimsical show,
Juggling my thoughts, they steal the glow.

But spillages happen, laughter's embrace,
Wipe it quick, wear the happy face.
Chasing the day with a silly grin,
Sky's the limit when fun begins!

Savoring Simple Moments

A quiet nook where comfort thrives,
Warm aromas and laughter arrives.
Pastries whisper, "Take a bite,"
Joy in crumbs, oh what a sight!

Sandwich made with love's own hand,
Each morsel thrown like grains of sand.
Sharing secrets with a bright-eyed mate,
In silly voices, we speculate.

A glance exchanged, a cheeky smile,
Time slows down, let's sit a while.
Between the bites, we laugh and sigh,
In these moments, we learn to fly.

Stirring the pot of sweet delight,
We cherish the day, from morn to night.
In simple things, happiness grows,
Laughter sips from the heart's open flows.

Beneath the Steamy Surface

In bubbles rise, a mystery brews,
Warmth embraces, I can't refuse.
Whimsical swirls in a porcelain cup,
The world outside can wait, and hush up.

Each sip sends giggles far and wide,
Funny faces, just can't hide.
Stirring stories with silken cream,
Beneath the steam, we plot and dream.

Frothy clouds drip their secrets low,
Conversations spark, bubbling slow.
A dash of humor, a splash of cheer,
Together we toast, with nothing to fear.

Time ticks by, yet we stand still,
Caught in moments, what a thrill!
In a swirl of laughter, our hearts take flight,
Within these sips, we find the light.

Twinkling Eyes over Toasted Treats

With every crunch, a giggle pops,
Butter drips, and joy never stops.
Coffee splashes, smiles abound,
In crumbs of laughter, we are found.

A toast to mornings, bright and keen,
McMuffin dreams, a breakfast scene.
Jams and jests, we spread with glee,
Together, sipping, just you and me.

Croissants flake, as chuckles rise,
The aroma dances, oh what a surprise!
We nibble slowly on whimsy bites,
In a café filled with warm delights.

Jokes over pastries, sweet and light,
With every sip, our hearts take flight.
With twinkling eyes, we share the feast,
In a world of joy, we're laughter's beast.

Tiny Joys in a Gigantic World

In a sea of chaos, small things shine,
A tiny cup, a drop of brine.
Every smile, a spark on high,
Making clouds of worries fly.

Giggles in sidewalks, hopscotch plays,
Colorful blooms in dusty bays.
With every spark, we hold the day,
Sipping wonder, come what may.

Chasing moments, bright and bold,
In the silly stories that are told.
Ferny plans and doughy dreams,
Under the sun, hear laughter's beams.

Out of the shadows, figures groove,
With little nudges, our spirits move.
Tickles in the air, you stop to say,
In a whirlwind of joy, let's seize the day!

Awakening Joy

Morning whispers in the light,
A mug in hand, it feels just right.
Beneath the surface, giggles hide,
Like caffeinated waves, they ride.

Steam rises, as froth takes form,
In every sip, there's playful charm.
A swirl of flavors, a dance for taste,
In every moment, none to waste.

Light breezes laugh through window seams,
Tickling thoughts, igniting dreams.
With every chuckle, the day takes flight,
In a teacup, soft as night.

Together brewing, hearts aligned,
In every moment, joy designed.
Our giggles bubble, profoundly shared,
With every sip, our souls prepared.

Brews of Bliss

An empty cup, a hint of cheer,
The world awaits, come gather near.
Caffeine giggles, a full embrace,
In whimsy's dance, we find our pace.

A sprinkle here, a swirl of fun,
Brewed warmth rising, two become one.
With playful hearts, we toast the day,
In cups of love, we laugh and play.

Whipped cream smiles, a playful mount,
Sip and laugh, an endless count.
From tiny sips to hearty swigs,
In every splash, joy always digs.

Amidst the froth, we chase delight,
Sprinkling hints of laughter's light.
We conquer mornings, one by one,
In togetherness, it's all such fun!

Sip, Savor, Smile

A swirl of cream, a dash of cheer,
Sip it slow, let worries disappear.
A giggle rides the frothy wave,
In every sip, new joy we crave.

A clink of mugs, good friends prevail,
Jokes as rich as the sweetened grail.
With every gulp, we fill our hearts,
Each moment cherished, fun imparts.

A sprinkle of sugar, a pinch of glee,
Caffeine-fueled chuckles, wild and free.
In cozy corners, laughter flows,
A comedy show where friendship grows.

So raise your cup, let spirits fly,
In this warm nook, we laugh, we cry.
With every slurp, the day feels bright,
Sip, savor, smile, all feels right.

Sweet Whispers in Comfy Cafés

In a cozy booth, whispers swirl,
Laughter dances, coffee's pearl.
The barista spins tales, hot and bold,
Each story richer than treasures of old.

With muffins smiling, and pastries on display,
We swap our secrets, let troubles stray.
A burst of chuckles with chocolate drips,
Life's little quirks, our fingertips.

The aroma wraps us, a warm embrace,
In this hideaway, we find our space.
Jokes bubble up like a brew that's bright,
With every sip, the world feels right.

Sweet whispers blend like cream in our drinks,
In charming cafés, we toast and think.
Moments of joy in every shared bite,
Here's to friendship, and laughter's delight!

A Dance of Foam and Friendship

Sipping softly, the foam takes flight,
A dance of bubbles, oh what a sight!
Jokes collide like espresso shots,
In the blissful clatter, laughter knots.

Stir up the fun with a smile or two,
Cupped hands gather secrets anew.
Each gentle sip, a ritual we share,
In this merry place, we don't have a care.

Caramel ribbons on cappuccino dreams,
Our little world flows like soft cream streams.
Tickled by humor that never gets old,
Friendship's a treasure more precious than gold.

So raise your mug, let the fiesta begin,
With every chuckle, we dance from within.
In a swirl of froth, we find our bliss,
In every cup, a hug, a sweet kiss.

Spiced Laughter in Every Corner

A pinch of spice, humor in the air,
Fortunes told by the latte fair.
With every sip, we crack a grin,
In this café, the fun won't thin.

The clock ticks slow, like a sip of cream,
In cozy corners, we plot and scheme.
A dash of mischief, a sprinkle of cheer,
Every joke lands, with friends near.

In the warmth of cups, our stories unfold,
With every pour, new plans are told.
Laughter echoes like a sweet refrain,
In spiced delights, we share our gain.

So gather 'round, let the good times roll,
In every corner, we nourish the soul.
With laughter brewed strong, our spirits soar,
In this café haven, we always want more.

Mugfuls of Happiness

In the morning sun, a brew so bright,
Sipping stories, feels just right.
With a dash of cream, the world's a game,
A frothy smile, insanity to tame.

Laughter bubbles in a cup so round,
Steam whispers secrets, joy abound.
With every sip, my worries fade,
Coffee's magic, an endless parade.

Friends gather close, sharing a tale,
Like wobbly spoons set to sail.
Chuckle and sip, spill a bit here,
Adventures brewed, with nothing to fear.

As the mugs clink, we toast to the day,
Unfiltered moments in a playful way.
Who needs a plan when we've got this treat?
One more espresso and it's all so sweet.

Frothy Dreams and Sweet Serenity

Whipped cream clouds on a bright brown lake,
Bubbly joy in every wake.
A sprinkle of sugar, the world gets light,
Dancing swirls in the morning bright.

Tickle the tongue with flavors that sing,
Each sip a flight, on caffeinated wings.
Laughter escapes with each happy sip,
Floating through moments, let's not let it slip.

With friends around, contentment in view,
We tell silly tales and sip something new.
Frothy dreams, like cream, rise above,
In every mug, there's a hint of love.

So here's to the laughter that brews in our hearts,
To the joy found in cups, in trivial parts.
Life's silly moments taught us to play,
In frothy concoctions, we brighten the day.

A Serenade in a Sip

From the pot it pours, a bittersweet tune,
Morning serenade under the noon.
With every sip, a symphony plays,
Melodies of joy in the steamy haze.

A swirl of caramel, a hint of delight,
I dance with my mug, a heart taking flight.
Smiles perk up like bubbles in cream,
Every gulp is a whimsical dream.

Cloudy thoughts dissolve in a warm embrace,
With each little laugh, we find our place.
Together we sip, in jests we bond,
Chasing the clouds of a light-hearted pond.

So raise your cups to the moments we share,
In laughter and sips, nothing can compare.
Cheers to the froth and the joy it brings,
A tune in our hearts, that forever sings.

Aromas of Affection

The kettle whistles, a delightful call,
Steaming wonders that enchant us all.
A pinch of spice, a hug in a cup,
With every sip, we feel the light up.

Dancing bubbles on our lips do play,
Echoing giggles throughout the day.
Friends' faces glow with a sprinkle of cheer,
In this cozy nook, there's nothing to fear.

Chasing shadows with laughter so bright,
Overheating with joy, we'll sip through the night.
In this warm moment, all worries cease,
With each little smile, we find our peace.

So hold up your mugs, let the aromas swirl,
In this delightful dance, we give it a twirl.
A tapestry woven with flavors and fun,
In the heart of this brew, we're forever spun.

Aromatic Adventures

In the morning sun, we spill,
Coffee on our favorite frill.
A giggle here, a smile there,
Caffeine dreams dance in the air.

Stirring cups with wild designs,
We weave stories like fine wines.
With every sip, the world turns bright,
Brewing joy beneath daylight.

Frothy waves and playful sips,
Laughter bubbles from our lips.
Each sip, a joke, a gentle tease,
In this café, we find our ease.

So here's to mugs that never tire,
To frothy tops and hearts on fire.
With every blend, a bond so tight,
In aromatic charms, we ignite.

The Sweetness of Shared Moments

Underneath the bustling skies,
We share tales and endless pies.
Each bite a laugh, each laugh a grin,
A moment sweet that draws us in.

Three spoons in a caramel swirl,
Giggles leap, the flavors whirl.
From tiny cups, our spirits soar,
With every sip, we crave for more.

Creamy dreams and whispered cheer,
In every gulp, your joy I hear.
Together we blend, like brew and bean,
In amusing tales, we find our sheen.

So raise your cup, let friendship rise,
In every moment, laughter flies.
For in shared sips, we truly find,
A sweetness only hearts can bind.

Festive Brews and Friendly Faces

In the corner, laughter floats,
Wrapped in warmth like stylish coats.
Foamy hearts in every drink,
With chuckles sweet, we start to think.

Spilling stories with each pour,
Joking loudly, we want more.
Friendly faces, shining bright,
Fill the room with pure delight.

With knock-knock jokes and silly puns,
We celebrate, we're all just fun.
Cinnamon dust on chilly days,
In every stir, we find new ways.

So gather 'round, let's toast again,
To memories brewed with faithful friends.
In cozy moments, we embrace,
Joyful sips and warm-hearted grace.

A Heartfelt Brew

In the morning glow, we meet,
Chasing dreams with drinks so sweet.
Silly giggles lift the gloom,
As laughter fills the crowded room.

Sipping slow, we play our parts,
Mixing flavors with our hearts.
Every shot, a punchline dear,
In this space, we have no fear.

From spills to thrills, it's quite a show,
With every taste, our bonds do grow.
Hearts collide in steamy cheer,
Together, we make joy appear.

So raise your cup, let stories flow,
In every drink, our spirits grow.
For in this brew, we find our song,
A heartfelt blend where we belong.

Embracing the Ordinary

In the morning's gentle glow,
Socks mismatched, but spirits high,
A toast to the spills we share,
Between laughter and the pie.

Chasing dreams like wayward cats,
Falling in puddles, oh what a sight!
We juggle plans like paper hats,
Every blunder feels just right.

With each sip of warm delight,
We clink our cups, a cheer so bright,
Even the burnt toast can seem gold,
As we brave the tales we've told.

In this embrace of ordinary things,
We find the joy that kindness brings.

Mirthful Whispers

Whispers carried on the breeze,
Tickles hiding in the air,
With every giggle, a little tease,
Joy that dances everywhere.

Coffee spills become our fame,
Sipping slowly, we still smile,
With playful grins, we fan the flame,
And share our stories, all worthwhile.

The clock may tick, but we don't care,
Counting blessings, one by one,
Jumping puddles, without a care,
In this silly game, we run.

Mirthful whispers hold us close,
In our hearts, we find our prose.

Gossamer Moments in Cream

Swirling dreams in frothy foam,
A sprinkle of joy in each cuppa,
With giggles bright like sugar's dome,
Life's joys drift in sweet and fluffer.

Twirling spoons and playful games,
In a mug, our stories steep,
Each sip a chuckle, none the same,
In our laughter, memories leap.

A dance of cream, a swish of bliss,
As time melts away, oh, what a treat!
In gossamer moments, we can't miss,
Finding magic in each heartbeat.

Together we toast to whims untold,
In these moments, our lives unfold.

The Canvas of Comfort

On canvas bright, our lives are drawn,
With strokes of fun, each day anew,
Coffee rings like the rising dawn,
Brushes dancing, me and you.

Each splatter of joy is a tale we tell,
As colors blend, our spirits rise,
In chaos and giggles, we dwell,
Finding wonder in everyday skies.

With each sip, we color the grey,
Splashes of laughter on our way,
In this masterpiece, we breathe and play,
Creating art, come what may.

The canvas of comfort, bold and free,
In whimsical strokes, just you and me.

A Raft of Roasted Revelry

In a café bright and cheery,
People spill their tales so merry.
A cup of joy, a splash of cream,
Each sip ignites a waking dream.

Jokes fly high like frothy foam,
Laughter dances, finds a home.
With every chuckle, giggles bloom,
Our hearts expand, dispel the gloom.

Chocolate sprinkles on a cake,
Each bite brings smiles we can't fake.
A pie of whimsy on the plate,
Oh, how we celebrate our fate!

So raise your cup, hold it tight,
In this moment, all feels right.
With friends around and stories grand,
A roasted joy, all perfectly planned.

Mugs of Merriment and Musings

Gather 'round, the mugs are near,
Filled with warmth and tipsy cheer.
Whispers shared and chuckles bright,
Our silly tales take glorious flight.

With every sip, the tales get tall,
Like gingerbread men at a ball.
Sipping slow, then bursting loud,
We fill our hearts, a merry crowd.

The barista winks, adding spice,
A dash of joy, a sprinkle of nice.
Garrisoning giggles, laughter rings,
In cozy corners, friendship sings.

So clink your mugs, make a toast,
To the silly things we love the most.
With every blend, our spirits soar,
Mug in hand, who could ask for more?

Brewed Bliss Beneath the Sky

Under the sun, we find our cheer,
Brewed delights, the best type of beer.
Clouds drift lazily in the blue,
Filled with daydreams fresh and new.

With each sip, the worries fade,
Tickled fancies, no charade.
A splash of cream, a dash of fun,
Watch as the silly stories run.

Friends gathered in the midday glow,
Sharing giggles, letting go.
Sunshine laughter, sweetened talk,
In this moment, time does walk.

So raise your glass to joy unbound,
In brewed bliss, love is found.
With happy hearts and grinning gleams,
Together we chase our wittiest dreams.

Froth-Filled Dreams and Delights

Frothy dreams in every cup,
Sipping slowly, never rushing up.
Swirls of cream and giggles blend,
Together we live, around the bend.

Whipped sugar, buttery treats,
Filling our lives in flavorful beats.
Fancies tickle like the lightest breeze,
In coffee corners, we find our ease.

Chasing whims of comedy bold,
Our stories shared, never old.
Every laugh like honey drips,
A symphony of joyful quips.

So linger long in this warm embrace,
With froth-filled dreams, we find our place.
In every giggle and every bite,
Delight blooms bright, a splendid sight.

www.ingramcontent.com/pod-product-compliance
Lightning Source LLC
Chambersburg PA
CBHW051638160426
43209CB00004B/696